GW00598405

Tricia

I do hope you will find this of some interest.

With love

John

The author is a retired hospital consultant with a particular interest in diseases of occupation. He also undertook studies to identify reasons for failed tuberculosis immunisation programmes.

One of his early junior hospital appointments was to a specialist ward at St Mary's Hospital, London, where pioneering treatment of tuberculous meningitis had commenced following the advent of the antibiotic Streptomycin.

He designed and had produced a simple, inexpensive, disposable vaccinating device which ensures accurate introduction of the vaccine Bacillus Calmette–Guérin (BCG) for protection against tuberculosis

As a result of these studies, he was appointed a member of the Joint Committee on Vaccination and Immunisation of the UK Department of Health. He was also asked by the South African government's Department of Health to review their immunisation programme against tuberculosis.

His commitment to his tuberculosis studies may well have been inspired by his own recovery from tuberculosis when a child. Before the advent of antibiotics, he spent two years in a sanatorium in order to overcome the disease.

He obtained his postgraduate doctorate degree as a result of the studies into the causes, other than flour, of respiratory allergy in flour mill workers.

His interests in retirement include recaning and restoring antique chairs, basket making and growing organic vegetables.

Dedication

To Maureen, my wife, for her patience and support.

Dr John A Lunn

MEMORIES OF A NATIONAL SERVICE DOCTOR

AUSTIN MACAULEY PUBLISHERS™

LONDON • CAMBRIDGE • NEW YORK • SHARJAH

Copyright © Dr John A Lunn (2018)

The right of Dr John A Lunn to be identified as author of this work has been asserted by him in accordance with section 77 and 78 of the Copyright, Designs and Patents Act 1988.

All rights reserved. No part of this publication may be reproduced, stored in a retrieval system, or transmitted in any form or by any means, electronic, mechanical, photocopying, recording, or otherwise, without the prior permission of the publishers.

Any person who commits any unauthorised act in relation to this publication may be liable to criminal prosecution and civil claims for damages.

A CIP catalogue record for this title is available from the British Library.

ISBN 9781788481823 (Paperback)
ISBN 9781788481830 (Hardback)
ISBN 9781788481847 (E-Book)
www.austinmacauley.com

First Published (2018)
Austin Macauley Publishers Ltd™
25 Canada Square
Canary Wharf
London
E14 5LQ

Acknowledgements

I am indebted to my daughters, Kate, Juliet and Joanna, for their invaluable technical help in assembling this book.

Chapter 1
National Service Background

In World War I, the British Army grew to 4 million, the greatest it has ever been. In World War II, without the dreadful attrition of trench warfare, the Army was not as great, and at its height in 1945 was 2.9 million.

In the post-war period tension with the USSR and defence of the Empire, apart from India which became independent in 1947, Britain still required a large army. In 1955, the year I began my National Service, the Army was a quarter of a million strong. A large contingent was stationed in Germany and much of the remainder scattered around the world in outposts of Empire. The Royal Army Medical Corps (RAMC) had difficulty recruiting enough regular doctors and relied on National Service recruits. For this reason, medical students were allowed to complete their training before doing their National Service.

I trained at St Mary's Hospital, Paddington, and qualified in December 1953. I completed my two mandatory house appointments in December 1954. I had received an excellent medical training, but nothing had prepared me for some of the events that lay ahead of me in the Army.

All young men who were required to do National Service, had to be medically examined to establish their fitness for enlistment. In early December 1954, I was informed that I had to go to the Queen Alexandra's

Military Hospital, Millbank, to have my medical examination. King Edward VII accompanied by Queen Alexandra first opened the hospital in 1905. It was a grand building with high ceilings and very long corridors. Potential recruits arrived at the examination centre in the hospital having had to walk along a very long corridor. I got the impression that the rather bored looking examining doctors considered that if you were able to walk that far, you were fit enough. The actual medical check was very cursory, and the only indication that I had passed was when I received my call-up papers at the end of December 1954.

The envelope with my call-up papers included instructions to proceed to Ash Vale Station, near Mytchett, Surrey. A railway warrant for the journey was included together with instructions regarding dress. A smart jacket and tie would be worn. It was also made clear which train I had to catch and that I would be met at Ash Vale Station accordingly.

On the appointed day in early January 1955, I stepped out of the train at Ash Vale Station and felt that I had then left the civilian world behind me. For the first time in my adult life, I realised that I would no longer be free to make my own decisions. An Army vehicle was waiting to take me to the nearby Keogh Barracks where the basic six weeks' training would take place.

There were just eight of us in this intake, and this enabled us soon to become good companions. Much of the six weeks consisted of learning about tropical diseases and hygiene, but some basic military skills were also instilled in us. This included marching, and one member of our group caused much amusement. He had a certain problem when it came to doing an 'about-turn'. Starting from stationary, he marched, as usual, with an arm going forward at the same time as the opposite leg. When it came to completing the 'about-turn' procedure, and we were facing the reverse direction, something seemed to get disconnected in his locomotory nervous system. Instead of marching off with an opposite arm and leg going forward, he would proceed to advance with his left arm and left leg both going forward together, and likewise, the right arm and leg. It was a most amusing sight and the group and instructing NCO always burst out laughing. No feelings were hurt, fortunately, and the recruit concerned was good-natured. He turned out to be one of the best of Army doctors in our group.

The regular Army NCOs who undertook our training were all extremely kind and tolerant of us, especially as our drill standard did not exactly match that of regular troops. We all became good friends with them, and we clubbed together at the end of the course to give them each a present.

The eight of us slept in a large wooden room, which was well heated by the Army coke burning stove. The weather was unusually cold in January 1955, but the heating was first class in keeping the room warm. One night, I was woken feeling excessively hot and the room was aglow with an orange light. The iron stove was glowing red hot and was lighting up the whole room. Somehow, when the stove had been made up last thing at night, the venting flap at the bottom had been accidentally left wide open. Once closed, the stove gradually settled down.

We were taught the etiquette expected of 'an officer and gentleman'. No swearing or too much drinking. In the mess we were always to return the newspaper we had read, neatly folded up back from where we had found it!

After a very happy six weeks, our group was photographed and I still have the photograph today. Before we dispersed, a form was put on the notice board with our names on. Against our names, we were invited to tick the appropriate column indicating whether we preferred a home posting or one abroad. As Maureen, my wife to be, and I had only just begun to know each other, I naturally ticked the column for a home posting. What a mistake! I was almost at once told I would be posted to the British Military Hospital in Fayid, Egypt. I had clearly failed to appreciate the Army way of thinking! Once we had all dispersed to our various postings, none of us ever met again, but I can still look at the photograph as a reminder of a very happy six weeks.

Chapter 2
Journey to Egypt

Long distance air travel was only just beginning in those days and was not the regular method of transport for long distances. The journey was, therefore, by sea. We joined our ship, the Empire Ken, at Southampton. I had never been on a sea voyage before, and this was obviously a great experience. Its novelty offset some of the apprehension at my posting being so far away from home.

We had a fine view of the Rock of Gibraltar as the ship turned into the Mediterranean. The ship had one stop en route at Algiers. We were not allowed to disembark there because of the Algerian uprising against the French colonial occupiers at that time. It was considered too dangerous, as we would have almost certainly been targets for those opposing the French.

After a twenty-four hour stop at Algiers, we proceeded on our way to Egypt. In the evenings there was usually entertainment on board, often bingo. On one such occasion, I had extraordinary good fortune and got the winning numbers three times. On the final time, I did not collect my winnings, as I thought the other ranks might think I had some magic dodge in order to win three times!

On the tenth day of the voyage, when looking out of the porthole on waking in the morning, instead of looking at the sea, we were alongside the stone quayside wall at Port Said, moored ready for disembarkation. The ship's docking had taken place, unnoticed while we were asleep, and came as a surprise.

On leaving the ship, an Army lorry was waiting to take me along seventy miles or so of the Suez Canal road to reach the British Military Hospital at Fayid.

Before leaving England, we had been warned of the need of becoming exposed to the sun very gradually, a maximum of five minutes a day to start with, and increased by that amount each day. It was as well to have followed this advice. Some did not and became severely sun burnt.

I was allocated to the dysentery ward at the hospital, not the most exciting commitment, but in fact some sufferers became extremely ill, and had to have intravenous drips to avoid serious dehydration. Another concern was that an occasional case of appendicitis masqueraded as dysentery, and it was essential to check patients very carefully, as it was all too easy to assume everyone in the ward had dysentery.

One evening when acting as duty medical officer, a report came through that one of the East African Pioneer Corps soldiers in a nearby camp had had a mental breakdown. His breakdown had resulted in him becoming extremely violent. The poor soldier had received some tragic news from his home in East Africa. His grief was compounded by the fact that, being so far away from his home, he could not make any contact with his family.

We awaited the arrival of the ambulance and as it approached we could hear loud banging and shouting. He was clearly being very violent and out of control. We opened the back ambulance doors, and two of our strongest soldiers managed to restrain him sufficiently to enable me to give him an intramuscular injection of 10 ml of paraldehyde. Paraldehyde is a sedative and was given in the hope that the patient would begin to feel calmer and settle down. After an appropriate time to allow the injection to work, it became evident that no calming effect was going to happen. The patient was an extremely large individual and given the violence of the situation, I decided that a further injection of paraldehyde was necessary and duly gave it. Calmness began to prevail and we were able to get the patient out of the ambulance and into a hospital bed.

The next morning, I went to the ward to see how the poor bereaved soldier was. He was sleeping very peacefully but the whole ward smelt of paraldehyde. The drug is exhaled through the lungs. The Army psychiatrist happened to be present and he told me that I should never have given the soldier two injections of the sedative. I said nothing but wished he had been on call the previous evening to witness how violent and dangerous the patient had been and how ineffective the one injection was.

The Officers' Mess consisted of regular and National Service doctors. Unfortunately, some National Service doctors were very bitter at being in the Army and were often rude to, and resentful of, the regular officers. So much so, that regular and National Service officers sat on separate tables for meals, a highly regrettable situation.

It was quite pleasant to walk out in the desert behind the hospital, and on one occasion I came across a cactus plant, quite on its own and with a delightful little flower. The words in Gray's Elegy: "Full many a flower is born to blush unseen, and waste its sweetness on the desert air", came to mind.

On another occasion, I was required to accompany an Army lorry taking goods across the desert road to Suez. The road was dusty, and hot, and in the middle of nowhere we came upon a little hut in which an Egyptian was selling tins of lemonade. I got out of the lorry and bought some. When coming to pay, I only had a large denomination note, and the Egyptian did not have enough change to give me. I went to put the tins back, but he insisted on me having them for nothing! This, I did, but looking back on this incident, I should have insisted on him having the large denomination note without me having any change. I could have afforded to let him have it, far more than he probably could have afforded to give me the lemonade.

The military hospital was situated about a mile inland from the Great Bitter Lake. Our routine duties were usually completed in the morning, leaving the afternoons free for recreation. We often took the opportunity at this time to walk to the shore of the lake to swim. This was not always very idyllic, as ships passing through the Suez Canal discharged waste material into the lake, and, at times, it was possible while swimming to be surrounded by pieces of ships' waste material floating on the surface, some of which is best left unmentioned!

One afternoon when approaching the lake, instead of the usual blue sky, there appeared to be a low dark cloud stretching as far as could be seen out of sight to the right, and equally as far as could be seen to the left. On getting closer, it could be seen that it was a swarm of locusts. I had heard of such events but had never imagined that a swarm could be so massive. The local Egyptian farmers were outside, banging drums and dustbin lids with sticks, hoping to prevent the locusts descending on their crops. The swarm continued on into the far distance to the relief of these farmers, but obviously other farmers further away in the path of the swarm would lose all their crops when the locusts descended.

The Army chaplain was a constant help and support, and often arranged social events. An outstanding one was a trip to the pyramids and Cairo museum. It was a wonderful opportunity to see the Great Pyramid of Giza, the oldest of the Seven Wonders of the World.

The Great Pyramid of Giza, sometimes, but less often, called Cheops, is the largest of a complex of three pyramids. It was completed in 2560 BC, and took at least twenty years to complete. Some authorities claim it may have taken thirty years before it was finally built. It is 481 feet high, and for about 3800 years remained the tallest man made structure on earth. Its base covers an area of just over thirteen acres. Two and a half million limestone blocks were required to complete the pyramid. Each block weighed 2.5 tonnes, and was carved into perfect proportions with an accuracy of a fraction of an inch. The size of the central King's Chamber was too great for it to have been put in after the pyramid was completed, as it would have been too large to pass through the narrow entrance passageway. It had to be placed in position before the main building was started. The corner blocks of the pyramid were joined by a ball and socket system which in some way guarded against disturbance from earthquakes and heat expansion.

The outer mantle of the pyramid was covered with 144,000 highly polished white limestone blocks, which gave a brilliant, shiny outer covering to the pyramid. The light reflected from the sun gave a dazzling light, which could be seen many miles away, and if anyone was there, it was said, as far away as the moon! The pyramid shone like a jewel.

The shiny blocks on the outer surface were remarkable, not only because of their size and weight, but also because of the extraordinary accuracy of their construction. Each was perfectly flat and over six feet thick. Unfortunately, the pyramids do not have this wonderful outer brilliance today, as the limestone blocks were removed in the Middle Ages for use in the construction of mosques and other buildings.

The mortar used to secure the stone blocks was stronger than the stones it fixed. Although some of the mortar components have been identified, its exact composition has never been fully identified.

The Ancient Egyptians possessed such outstanding skills and ingenuity in building the pyramids that it is unlikely that they could be repeated today. It is impossible to understand how they achieved such wonders. They had a genius not known today.

The inner chambers were filled with large quantities of gold, jewels and a wide range of food and drink, as it was believed that these would be a comfort to the king in the afterlife. In subsequent centuries, it became well known that vast treasures were in the inner pyramid chambers and these were taken by grave robbers.

It has been said that the architect who designed and built the secret inner chamber of the pyramid, was killed when the building was completed; in order to maintain the secrecy of the inner king's chamber with all its priceless treasures. It must be presumed that the architect was not aware of this clause in his contract when undertaking the commitment to construct the pyramid.

The afternoon was spent in Cairo museum, and among the many outstanding displays, perhaps the greatest was the sarcophagus of King Tutankhamun, a massive structure of pure gold. On a historical note, the king's tomb was discovered in the Valley of the Kings by the great Egyptologist, Howard Carter in 1922.

Howard Carter was a well-known Egyptologist. His patron was Lord Carnarvon who enabled Carter to finance his expeditions. Carter was well aware that it was believed that all the pyramids had already been robbed of their treasures. He was, however, convinced that the tomb of Tutankhamun remained undisturbed, and on 4th November 1922, he made his remarkable discovery of the King's undisturbed burial chamber with all its treasures intact.

It was said that a curse would be put on anyone finding and disturbing Tutankhamun's chamber. A few months after Howard Carter's discovery, his patron, Lord

Carnarvon, died from an infected insect bite. This may have satisfied the curse as Howard Carter lived for many years longer.

Chapter 3
Recreation in Egypt

It has already been mentioned that the Army in Egypt was essentially a holding one. There were few entirely military activities. Medical officers at the British Military Hospital, Fayid, apart from in the acute dysentery ward, also had little to do, as the Army personnel were generally fully fit. When the morning medical duties had been completed, unless acting as the duty medical officer, afternoons were free for recreation. The officers' mess situated on the shore of the Great Bitter Lake was the usual, and essentially only, place to resort to.

During World War II, some German prisoners of war were kept in the Egyptian Canal Zone. They had the opportunity to undertake various activities, and one of their achievements was to build a small sailing boat. It is unlikely that they had many tools or materials for this, but with characteristic national skill and ingenuity they made a delightful little dinghy.

I had always wanted to learn to sail, and one of the regular Army officers who went to the officers' mess at the lake was a proficient sailor. He very kindly taught me. At times, I would sail out on the lake with a companion, but more often than not, on my own. The Great Bitter Lake is sufficiently large that it is not possible to see the far side, and when standing on the edge it is possible to imagine being at the seaside. For much of the day, the lake's water is calm. This can change quite rapidly late in the afternoon when a strong wind invariably starts coming from the lake towards the shore. The explanation for this is that hot air that has accumulated during the day from the desert rises late in the day and allows cooler air from over the lake to come on shore, which causes the familiar late afternoon winds. When out sailing, I always tried to return to the shore before the wind got up but on one occasion I lost track of the time and was well out in the lake when the wind began. I went about in the dinghy, but as I did so, the starboard shroud snapped, thus removing support for the mast from that side of the boat. Good fortune prevailed, as having just turned onto a port tack the wind was carrying the dinghy straight back to the shore. It was possible to reach the shore anchorage while remaining on the same tack. The broken starboard shroud was not the disaster it might have been.

Many years after I had left the Army, our neighbour and I were chatting about our National Service experiences. He had also been posted to the Egyptian Canal Zone, but being a few years older than me had been there some years earlier. At that time some of the German prisoners of war had still not been repatriated. He, like I had, learnt to sail in the same dinghy. His tutor was a German U-boat commander. A quite unique and distinguished tutor to teach one to sail.

One human tragedy my neighbour recounted was that some of the German prisoners of war in Egypt did not want to return to Germany. They had lost their families and homes due to the Allied bombing and had nowhere to return to. The Germany they had known did not exist anymore for them. During the war, we talked of "the enemy", but after the war, it could become a human tragedy and great sadness, no matter what anyone's nationality.

Chapter 4
Ain Sukhna

Ain Sukhna is a holiday resort lying on the western shore of the Gulf of Suez. It is approximately 55 kilometres south of the city of Suez. Cairo lies 120 kilometres eastward of the town. In relatively recent times, at least ten luxury hotels have been built there and Ain Sukhna is now a great attraction for tourists. In addition to hotel and town development, there is now a modern seaport.

Late in the twentieth century, archaeologists discovered evidence of an ancient civilisation at the site of the modern town, dating as far back as 2400 BC. They found that large galleries had been carved into the sandstone mountains lying a short distance from the sea. It was from inscriptions found on the walls of these galleries that the time of the original settlements was confirmed. It is likely that the galleries were used for living accommodation, trading and storage.

In 1955, there had been none of today's developments, and only vague indications of some of the ancient galleries carved in the mountain's sandstone. There were no buildings, just unspoilt sandy beaches and a clear blue sea.

As has previously been mentioned, the British Army in 1955 was merely a holding one and there was little to do. Ideas were sought as to how to pass the time and see some of the wonderful sites of Egypt. It was decided that a visit to Ain Sukhna was something we should not miss.

Somehow an official reason for a visit was dreamt up so that the entire venture could be undertaken in Army transport. Land rovers and trailers were made ready. Tents for shade, water and food supplies were packed in the trailers. In order that the expedition could be recorded as being official, and therefore necessary, it was called 'a much needed hygiene inspection'. No one ever queried this quite absurd excuse for the trip.

The journey from Fayid to Ain Sukhna was nearly 100 kilometres and took just over two hours to complete. On arriving, the tents were pitched on the beach not only to provide shade but also cover for changing into swimming costumes. A short distance off the shore the most beautiful coral could be seen. Something of beauty hard to describe.

Fragmented coral has very sharp edges, and we soon found it was necessary to wear protective sandals when entering the sea. One of the party failed to do so and it was extremely difficult to remove a piece of coral that had pierced the sole of his foot.

After an inspiring day, the expedition returned to Fayid, and to our surprise, we never had to account for what we had found or achieved during our hygiene inspection.

My memory of Ain Sukhna is of an unspoilt area of sand and clear blue sea. Just a slight indication of an ancient civilisation given from impressions in the mountain's sandstone, later known to be identified as the galleries dating back to 2400 BC.

It is hard to imagine now that this tranquillity and beauty has been transformed into a modern, Western-style holiday resort. Some would call it "progress".

Chapter 5
Ammunition Depot at Abu Sultan

After about six months in Fayid, I was posted as the medical officer on LST, Sir Humphrey Gale, a tank landing ship, sailing from Port Said down the Suez Canal and along the Red Sea, then turning up the Gulf of Aqaba in order to offload Army equipment for the Jordanian Army. At the top of the gulf, there was a simple stone jetty surrounded by palm trees. A truly delightful Arabian scene, but now I believe developed in Western style, even with a Hilton Hotel! A tragedy to destroy such a beautiful and tranquil spot.

The reason for there being a medical officer on this trip was because previously, a soldier had died from heat stroke on this voyage. The absurdity of having a doctor on board in case of further problems was that there was no resuscitation equipment on board so nothing could have been done to save anyone at risk of heatstroke.

The British Army was still supplying the Jordanian Army in 1955 because of a long-standing friendship between Britain and Jordan. A British general, John Bagot Glubb, later to be knighted, became very committed to establishing the Transjordan Arab League as an effective fighting force. The League was started in 1939, and at first only the Bedouin tribesmen were recruited. John Glubb adored and respected the Bedouin tribesmen, and considered that only they were the true Arabs. They were the only recruits he really wanted in the League. He dressed in Bedouin costume and spoke fluent Arabic. He became the commanding general of the League and was known as Glubb Pasha, the chief. As he adored the Bedouin, so they also respected and adored him. It was a wonderfully effective fighting force, and was a significant factor in adding to and strengthening the Jordanian Army. His command of the League ended in 1956, when his services were no longer considered necessary by the Jordanian Army.

The Gulf of Aqaba is lined on both sides by desert hills with no sign of vegetation or trees. A completely bleak landscape. On my third and last voyage to Aqaba, the Sir Humphrey Gale had to reload some equipment which had to be taken back to Egypt for repair. This allowed me some time to take some exercise and walk into some of the nearby hills. I had not gone far before an old Arab, dressed in the traditional Arab way, came walking towards me. He stopped, and in sign language indicated that he was inviting me to return with him to be given some hospitality. It was a true and wonderful Arab friendship. Unfortunately, being on my own and only having a limited time before the ship would be sailing, I had to decline his kindness. It was difficult to indicate why I had to do so and I just hoped I had not offended him, the very last thing in the world I would have wanted to do.

After three trips on the tank-landing ship, Sir Humphrey Gale, I was posted to an ammunition depot at Abu Sultan, which was protected by a Guards unit. I lived in an Army tent and found great tranquillity in it. The Guards officers were all extremely friendly to me, and this posting was one of the happiest times in the Army.

One tragedy happened while there. Egyptian labourers were hired to handle the ammunition cases etc. and a small railway was established to transport the ammunition across the desert to and from the storage sites. One morning, I had an urgent call, one of the labourers had slipped between the diesel engine and a truck and had been crushed to death. Each labourer just turned up every day in the hope of work, no one knowing their name or where they came from. As a result of this, it was impossible to know what to do with the body or who to notify. Some poor family would have lost their husband and father, never knowing under what circumstances, or having the body returned. I did not know what to do with the body and, enclosed in a body bag, got it transported down to the BMH at Fayid. Not long afterwards, I received a not unexpected, extremely irate call from the BMH duty medical officer, asking me what on earth I expected him to do with the body. I said I didn't know, but told him not to return it to me, and fortunately, he did not. It was a great tragedy and some family was never to know what happened to the husband and father.

The sad death of the Egyptian labourer was not the only deeply concerning event among the group of Egyptians working for the British Army. Severe diseases were all too common, and unfortunately, it was not within the RAMC's brief to provide treatment. It was often very hard for all in the RAMC medical unit at Abu Sultan to see and leave such illness untreated. On one occasion, it was impossible to allow a poor sufferer to be ignored. He was brought to me by an Egyptian comrade giving him much needed support. Looking at his face I saw something I had never seen before, and doubt and hope I never will again. A large area of the right side of his face had been eroded away by what appeared to be an infection. The cheekbone had disappeared completely so that the underlying maxillary sinus was exposed. This had made a crater-like defect of quite alarming proportions. There were no skilled investigations available to establish whether uncontrolled infection had caused the erosion or whether it might have been a cancerous growth. The whole of the cavity was heavily infected however, whatever the underlying cause. If the infection could be improved then the full diagnosis might be possible.

At that time, antibiotics had only recently become available. I did have a limited supply. I don't think any other doctor would have done other than what clearly had to be done. The cavity was cleaned as far as possible and covered with a dressing. The patient was started on a course of antibiotics. It was not easy to explain the need to take the treatment regularly, as he and his companion spoke no English. One of our medical orderlies, however, was a past master at communicating without language. He was able to make it quite clear how the antibiotics were to be taken. The patient also understood that I needed to see him the next day, and he did return. Likewise the day following, and it was heartening to see some slight reduction in the infection. Then sadness. He did not come the next day, or the next or ever again. Whatever happened to this desperately sick man, will never be known.

Chapter 6
Water Supplies

Living in the United Kingdom, water is something that is taken for granted, either when it comes out of a tap, or from the sky. When the Army established the Base Ammunition Depot at Abu Sultan (9 BAD) in the Egyptian desert, there was of course no water available. The ingenious Royal Electrical and Mechanical Engineers (REME) were able to establish a supply. They built a filtering and sterilising plant on the edge of the Sweet Water Canal and laid a pipeline across the desert to supply water to 9 BAD.

The medical unit at 9 BAD had a hygiene corporal attached, whose functions included carrying out a daily check on the chlorine levels in the water being conveyed in the pipe running across the desert. The acceptable chlorine level to ensure that water is safe to drink is within the range of 0.2–1.0 mg per litre. I do not remember the exact level the engineers decided on, but it was important to check daily that the established level had not dropped. If there was a drop in the level it almost certainly indicated that the water supply had been contaminated, and was not safe to drink. One morning, the hygiene corporal came to me greatly concerned because his estimation of chlorine that day had shown a marked drop in the chlorine. The level recorded indicated that the water could not be considered safe to drink, and the commanding officer was informed of this.

The introductory training we had back in the UK was now to prove how valuable it had been. We checked with the Royal Engineers at the filtering and sterilising plant that nothing had gone wrong there and soon had confirmation that it had not. The hygiene corporal and I then set out to walk across the desert to trace the water supply pipe for any faults. We had walked for at least half a mile, when in the distance a dark area in the sand could be seen surrounding the pipe. When we reached the area it was clear that the pipe had somehow become damaged and, in addition to water leaking out, it was also allowing contamination to enter the pipe. It was a relief, and satisfying, that the cause of the drop in the chlorine level had been identified. The Royal Engineers were informed, and by the end of the day, the pipe was mended and the water made safe to drink.

For the hygiene corporal, this was a significant 'pat on the back'. Having carried out the chlorine checking day after day without any variation, his conscientious checking had resulted in the prevention of a possible outbreak of waterborne disease.

Chapter 7
Parasites and Khamsin

The lectures we received during our initial training included valuable knowledge about diseases occurring in hot climates. Most of these diseases are not seen in the UK and I had no practical experience of them. This was soon to change.

Schistosomiasis or Bilharzia is an infection caused by a parasitic worm, the larvae of which swim in fresh water. The so-called Sweet Water Canal running alongside the Suez Canal was a potent source of this parasitic infection. The Sweet Water Canal obtained its name, rather misleadingly, because it was not salt water unlike the Suez Canal. The water was in fact far from sweet, as it was used for many human functions.

The life cycle of the parasite is quite complicated. Infected humans excrete the eggs, which can find their way into fresh water. Once there, the eggs hatch into larvae. The larvae seek out snails and enter them. They multiply in the snail and change into larvae called Cercariae. These leave the snail and return back into the water. They will penetrate the skin of any person going into the water and enter their blood stream. Once the Cercariae have entered the blood stream, they mature into adult worms. The worms invade various organs of the body, the liver, kidney and bladder being the commonest. The worms lay eggs, many of which will be excreted in the urine. Where there is no main sanitation, the eggs often find their way back into fresh water for the life cycle to begin again.

Troops were warned of the dangers of acquiring this parasite, and I am not aware that any from the UK ever did. Unfortunately, this was not the case with troops in the East African Pioneer Corps. It is possible that they had acquired the infection back in their own countries. On several occasions, some would come with symptoms strongly suggesting infection with the parasite, the main one being passing blood in the urine. When this stage is reached, the parasites have almost certainly been entrenched in the body for a considerable time. Once the bladder has been invaded, thickening and fibrosis of the wall can occur, and in some cases, this may be a prelude to the lesions becoming cancerous.

Treatment in 1955 involved giving Antimony in various forms of its chemical compounds. It was always a worrying treatment to give, as Antimony can create very toxic side effects. Several of the unfortunate sufferers with advanced Schistosomiasis of the bladder had a very poor prognosis. Today, the parasite is readily treated with Praziquantel, an extremely effective drug with minimal side effects.

In late July, we were given warning that a khamsin (a desert sand storm) was expected within the next twenty-four hours. We were warned that this would cause fine dusty sand to become airborne, and that anything exposed would become covered in it. I took the appropriate precautions with my possessions in the tent. The khamsin duly arrived and the air became like a thick London fog. Fine sand penetrated into the tent, leaving a film on every exposed surface, and somehow got into my suitcase even though it was firmly shut.

When the storm subsided, it took a considerable time to shake everything in the tent, free from the sand – especially the bedding. It was quite interesting to hear the various expletives of the other tent occupiers as they began to shake the sand from their possessions too. The words "officer and gentleman" didn't readily come to mind!

Troops often swam in the Great Bitter Lake near to where the Sweet Water Canal flowed into it and a number of those swimmers started getting skin and ear infections. I had the water cultured at the BMH Fayid and the result showed a huge number of faecal organisms. I informed the Commanding Officer who at once banned all swimming. I was extremely unpopular, but it was the right decision.

Before finally being accommodated in a tent at the ammunition depot at Abu Sultan, I had temporary accommodation in a small room in a wooden building. The walls were formed with slatted wood. After my first night's sleep, I found that I was not the only occupant of the room. Around both my ankles there were numerous red, raised and itchy spots. I had had a night visitation from bed bugs. After a few days, I was given a tent for accommodation and only had this extra company for a short time.

Bed bugs spend the daytime secreted in crevices between wooden slats forming hut walls, and in the daytime cannot be seen. At night, they are attracted by the warmth of the occupant and attach themselves to the skin to obtain a free supply of blood which is their staple diet. The insects, apart from causing itchy spots, are not known to transmit any diseases and their company was not a matter of great concern.

Chapter 8
Driving Test

While on this posting, I was told that if you passed the Army driving test it would transfer to a UK one. One day, I went to the transport officer seeking lessons with a view to getting a licence. There was a small van and he asked me to get in, and I drove it around Ismailia on desert roads, avoiding camels, donkeys and goats etc. When we returned to his hut, I asked him when would I have my first lesson. He replied, "You've passed". I must be the only person to have passed their driving test not knowing they were taking it!

Towards the end of 1955, the British Army was to end its occupation of the Canal Zone, and the ammunition depots and supplies were to be handed over to Egyptian contractors. To protect the ammunition from being taken, the British had put a double perimeter wire fence around each site and anti-personnel mines placed in the sand between the two boundaries. During the course of time and with some strong winds, some of the mines had worked their way to the surface. Before handing over to the Egyptian contractors, we warned them not to touch any metal object protruding out of the sand. On the very first day of the handover, and there was an overlap before we left, an Egyptian labourer was brought in to me with the fingers blown off one of his hands. He had picked up one of the mines! I doubt that any of the contractors had bothered to warn him of the danger.

Before the British Army withdrew from the Canal Zone, the staff of the British Military Hospital at Fayid held a farewell dance. Although posted at Abu Sultan, I was invited to the event. We were required to be dressed as pirates. Towards the end of the evening there was an elimination dance, and my partner and I reached the last two pairs. To find the winner, each man had to sit on his partner's knee and be fed a bottle of milk. The winner of course was the one who finished the bottle first and this, with no credit attached, was myself. This gained me the dubious title of "Champion Sucker".

In early December 1955, I was due for a month's UK leave, not having had any during the year. By then, York aircraft were flying troops to and from the UK, and on such I returned home for my leave. The York had to stop en route at Malta but it was night time when it did; so although I have been to Malta, I have seen nothing of it as the York took off for home just after dawn the next day.

Chapter 9
Cyprus

Following my three weeks' leave in the UK in December 1955, I was posted to Cyprus. Prior to 1955, Cyprus had been the most tranquil and happy posting for Army personnel in the Middle East. That all began to change towards the end of 1955.

Cyprus is a delightful and beautiful island situated in the eastern Mediterranean but, rather sadly, its history has been one of subjugation by foreign empires over the centuries. One of the earliest of these was the Roman Empire, and some of the remains of their classic buildings can be seen near Famagusta.

Apart from a wide range of agriculture products, including many vineyards, the island has also been a rich source of copper for centuries. As long ago as 5000 BC there are reports of copper being mined. The name of the island probably comes from either the Greek word for copper, Kypros or the Latin equivalent, Cuprum. The population of the island consists of approximately 82% Greek Cypriots and 18% Turkish. The Turkish Cypriots live mainly in the north of the island.

In 1878, a convention gave Great Britain the protectorate rights of the island. This was a transfer from the previous occupiers, the Ottoman Empire. The indigenous Greeks on the island were never happy with this agreement and wanted to have union with Greece, Enosis.

In 1914, Great Britain offered to cede Cyprus to Greece if Greece would attack Bulgaria. Greece did not agree to this, and in 1925, Cyprus was declared a Crown Colony. The Greeks, however, increasingly wanted Enosis. It was against this background that the movement to oust the British began. The organisation established to do this was called Ethniki Organosis Kyprion Aghoniston (EOKA) and was masterminded by Colonel Dighenis Grivas. The English translation of the full wording for EOKA is 'The National Organisation of the Cypriot Struggle'. By the end of 1955, EOKA was beginning its campaign of armed violence against the occupying British Forces.

It was against this background of the start of the EOKA campaign that I received my posting to Cyprus early in January 1956. Once again I flew by York aircraft. The York had been developed from a World War II bomber and had very few comforts. It was cold and extremely noisy. My posting in Cyprus was to the British Military Hospital, Nicosia, which became the centre for treating the casualties from the EOKA campaign. The day before leaving the UK for this posting the papers reported that a bomb had exploded outside the officers' mess at the hospital, so I had some awareness of what lay ahead. Fortunately, no injuries occurred from this incident.

Once settled in my new surroundings, I discovered that a very pleasant aspect in the officers' mess was the warm and cordial relations between the Regular and National Service officers. This was in marked contrast to Egypt where because the 'holding' Army had nothing to do, there had been nothing to bond the two groups of officers together. In Cyprus, the grim results of the EOKA campaign and the many badly wounded soldiers meant we all had to work together. Two of the Regular officers, once I had left the Army, even came to Maureen's and my wedding.

The surgical team at the hospital was led by the late Colonel John Watts, a most distinguished war surgeon. He had performed wonderful feats in treating the wounded in World War II and also in the subsequent Korean War. On many occasions, he had risked his life to reach and operate on wounded soldiers. His experience was second to none in treating war wounds, and we were very fortunate to have had the privilege of knowing him and working with him. A wonderful inspiration, and memories of him will never be forgotten by all those who knew him.

Chapter 10
Maureen and Happy Times

The northern part of Cyprus was mainly populated by Turkish Cypriots who of course had no desire for Enosis. It was fairly safe for British troops, when on leave, to visit some recreational areas in northern Cyprus. In spite of the EOKA campaign requiring medical personnel to be on duty much of the time, it would be wrong to suggest that there were no opportunities to have some off-duty time and relax.

In 1954, during my second hospital appointment, before starting my National Service, the charge nurse on the ward, Maureen Marshall and I became good friends. After my first Army year in Egypt, leave was granted and this allowed me to return to the UK. Maureen and I were able to meet again and strengthen our friendship.

When my leave was over at the end of December 1955, it was very hard to say goodbye to Maureen when starting my second year of National Service in Cyprus. Fortunately, it was not to be another year before we saw each other again. A copper mining company, The Cyprus Mines Corporation working at Xeros in the north west of the island, had established a hospital for their workers and relatives. Maureen learnt that a nursing post had become vacant in the hospital. She successfully applied for this and six weeks after I had arrived in Cyprus, we were once again able to meet.

As Xeros was some distance from Nicosia, it was necessary to hire a Turkish Cypriot owned taxi. Again good fortune prevailed. Ian Sparling, another fellow National Serviceman, had bought a little Renault car. At short notice, before he had time to sell it, he was given a posting outside Cyprus. He asked me if I would look after his car and use it whenever I wished. This, of course made getting to and from Xeros much less difficult. I never heard from Ian Sparling again or knew where his new posting was. When my time came to leave the Army, I still had no knowledge of where he was and therefore was unable to know what he wanted me to do with the car. The car keys were left with the hospital adjutant and the car under a tree for shade. To this day, I have never been able to make contact with Ian Sparling. I only hope he managed to have his car back but I shall never know.

With the benefit of the car, Maureen and I were able to meet much more readily. A favourite meeting place was at Newman's Farm near Kyrenia. Mr and Mrs Newman owned a dairy herd, and just outside their farmhouse were trees beneath which tables and chairs were placed. Mrs Newman produced delicious cream teas and ice-cold milk shakes. Maureen and I, on several occasions, enjoyed not only Mrs Newman's wonderful cream teas, but also the cool provided by the shade of the trees. We also, of course, enjoyed each other's company!

Andrew Thornton, another medical National Serviceman working as an anaesthetist at the Military Hospital, became engaged to a delightful girl, Elizabeth, who worked for the British government in premises attached to the British Military Hospital in Nicosia. Elizabeth's mother also lived in Cyprus, and Elizabeth and Andrew decided to be married in Cyprus while he remained in the Army. I was very honoured when Andrew asked me to be his best man. To be asked was another unexpected event in my time in the Army. Andrew, in later life, became godfather to our youngest daughter, Joanna.

Our visits to Newman's Farm were sometimes preceded by a visit to a cove called Donkey Beach. The cove was only a short distance further west from the farm. It was about twenty-five yards across and totally unspoilt. Whenever we went there, it was completely deserted.

Maureen had not been given swimming lessons of any significance before, and Donkey Beach provided a perfect opportunity for her to gain confidence in the water. The sea was crystal clear, and by swimming across the cove close to the shore, it was always easy to avoid being out of her depth. While we were in the water, my revolver had to be left under cover beneath our picnic blanket. No one ever came to Donkey Beach while we were there, and this was just as well given the foolishness of being away from the weapon. With these ideal conditions, Maureen became very confident and made great progress with her swimming.

After swimming, we climbed rocks close to the cove to have a picnic. I had acquired a Primus stove during my time in Egypt and with this, and the eggs Maureen always brought, I learnt how to make scrambled eggs. To this day, sixty years later, I still make the scrambled eggs, just about the total of my cooking skills.

The Dome Hotel in Kyrenia overlooked the idyllic harbour and also provided a happy meeting place for Maureen and myself. Our friendship continued to grow, and on one very happy meeting we became engaged to be married. As the main shopping areas of Nicosia were too dangerous and out of bounds to the Army, we were not able to buy a suitable engagement ring. We were, however, able to contact a firm back in the UK who sold suitable rings to act as a temporary measure before buying a proper one once home. The ring we bought only had a Zircon stone in it but served well as a temporary token of our engagement.

The ring, in the years to come, although relegated from being the official engagement ring, had great sentimental value to us both. Sadly, when we had been married for a number of years, our house was burgled and among the items stolen was the Zircon ring. Although of little material value, its loss was a very sad event, which no insurance policy could ever repay.

Chapter 11
Patient Care and Protection

During the Cyprus emergency in 1956, every soldier was issued with a small four-page card giving clear instructions when it was permissible to use firearms. Medical officers had more limited rights in their use of firearms and had to be guided by the rules of the Geneva Convention.

In 1859 Henry Dunant, a Swiss citizen, was deeply concerned at the suffering of the wounded at the Battle of Solferino. Many of the wounded lay where they had fallen, unattended and often dying through lack of care. He made public his concerns, which led to the establishment of the Red Cross in Geneva. In 1864, further progress was made in setting standards for the care of the war-wounded. This was soon followed by the first Geneva Convention. In recognition of his work Henry Dunant became the joint recipient of the first Nobel Peace Prize in 1901.

On the 6 July 1906, a further conference established the principles of care, which all wounded soldiers, whether friendly or enemy, should receive. Thirty-five nations attended the convention, which became known as "The Convention for the Amelioration of the Condition of the Wounded and Sick in Armies in the Field."

In subsequent years, because of increasing evidence of war atrocities and ill treatment of prisoners, further additions were needed to the original Convention's principles. This led to a further Geneva Convention in

1949. In all, four conventions have been concluded after the 1949 convention. In more recent times, terrorist and other subversive activities have brought more complex matters to the fore, which required further discussions.

The four-page card issued to all soldiers indicated when it was legal for soldiers to fire their weapons. The first statement on the card was clearly worded: "Before you use force it is always your duty to assess the situation confronting you and to decide what degree of force is necessary. If having done this carefully and honestly, and you decide there is no alternative but to open fire, and you then do so, you will be doing your duty and acting lawfully whatever the consequences."

Some people, after I had left the Army, queried why, as a non-combatant, I had been issued with a revolver. The answer was of course that the Geneva Convention states that medical officers may use firearms to defend themselves and their patients. I never had occasion to use my revolver under these permitted circumstances I am glad to say.

Prior to being issued with our revolvers, we were given firing practice. When a revolver is fired in one hand without support from the other, the gun jolts upwards. This results in the bullet going higher than the aimed-at target. Guns can be steadied with the other hand to prevent this upward movement. If not steadied in this way, it is necessary to aim lower in order to hit the intended target.

Chapter 12
A Near Miss

Early in 1956, the EOKA campaign had not reached its full impact and it was considered safe to walk into the main shopping areas of Nicosia, Ledra Street in particular. I and a fellow National Serviceman, Philip Barker, had reasons to go to Ledra Street, I to buy a length of flex for a bedside lamp, and Philip to try and acquire the latest Elvis Presley record. Both seemingly harmless enough things to do. However, the visit nearly cost me my life, and to this day I reflect on how close that moment was.

To give some background, there were several small potteries in Cyprus making charmingly patterned pottery. On a background of white, green-turquoise patterns were painted. Usually these consisted of shapes similar to wide aster flower petals arranged in rows interspersed with horizontal lines and delicately arranged with little rows of circular turquoise dots. Suitably shaped items of pottery could be made into bedside lamps, with the lamp bulb fitment going neatly into the narrowed neck of the pot. The pots had not usually been made with a view to being made into bedside lamps, and there was no low down hole for the flex to be inside the pot before emerging at the bottom. The Royal Army Dental Corps came to the rescue by using a dental drill to make the appropriate opening. I hope it is now too long ago for me, and the dentist, to be charged with misappropriation of Army property!

So, one afternoon in early January, Philip Barker and I walked down to Ledra Street. I went to an electrical shop for the flex and Philip to buy his record. The electrical shop I found had a very wide space between the entrance and the shop counter. Fortunate in view of what was about to happen. I walked up to the counter and almost at once a man came from a door behind the counter to ask what I wanted. I said I would like to have six feet of flex suitable for a table lamp. He nodded and disappeared through the door he had come from. After some considerable time waiting for him to return, I became impatient and happened to look up at the wall ahead of me behind the counter. There, clearly displayed, were all the flexes. I at once became alarmed and turned round to face the shop entrance. As I did so, two men wearing mackintoshes and with their hands in their pockets were about to enter the shop. On seeing me facing them they immediately swivelled and walked rapidly away. They had undoubtedly been alerted by the shop owner that here was a British 'sitting duck' waiting for them, and had hoped to commit one of many killings yet to come.

Little could they have known that I was in fact unarmed, and fortunately their weapons were not in a position to be fired while in their pockets.

I immediately left the shop without the flex and soon met Philip Barker where he was buying his records. We walked back to the safety of the British Military Hospital without contemplating any more shopping.

Shortly after this incident, several Army personnel were killed in Ledra Street and the whole of Nicosia was then put out of bounds to British troops. While in Cyprus, I was never able to complete the bedside lamp, but did so once I returned to the UK. The lamp is still being used to this day.

Chapter 13
Accidents and A Tragic Game

During the first quarter of 1956, when the EOKA campaign was becoming increasingly effective, the death and casualty rates amongst British troops inevitably became much greater. One very unfortunate happening was the number of soldiers wounded, and sometimes killed, by accidental discharge of weapons. Whenever leaving their base all soldiers had to carry armed weapons and, naturally, when returning to their bases, their weapons were still loaded. Those who were armed with revolvers were at particular risk of causing casualties amongst their fellow soldiers because a fully loaded revolver, if accidentally dropped on the floor, could be detonated just by the firing pin vibrating against the bullet in line with the barrel.

During the first three months of 1956, we kept a careful count of how troops were wounded or tragically killed. A very disturbing fact was that very nearly as many were killed or wounded by accidental discharge of weapons, as were by the EOKA campaign.

In order to prevent many of these tragedies, instead of being allowed six bullets in our revolvers, we were only allowed five. The chamber in the revolving cylinder aligned with the barrel had to be the one without a bullet. This did not reduce the effectiveness of the revolver because when the trigger is pulled the bullet in line with the barrel moves to the right and the bullet which fires is the one which was lying in the chamber to the left of the barrel. By enforcing only five bullets for a revolver, it meant that if it was accidentally dropped no bullet was discharged. It may seem strange that anyone should drop a weapon, but when removing a revolver from its holster after a hot and weary day, it was at times possible to let it slip out of the hand. Once the five only bullet rule was brought in, the number of accidental tragedies dropped significantly.

As already mentioned at the beginning of the book, nothing in my medical education had prepared me for much of what was to happen in the days ahead when doing my National Service. One such event occurred one morning, when I was just about to have a familiar and routine cup of coffee. A young corporal came rushing in saying a soldier had been shot and killed in the Army canteen. I hurried back with the corporal, mystified as to what had happened and hardly believing that the tragedy could have been caused by any EOKA activity. The sad truth was that the poor soldier had shot himself in a most bizarre way. He was, apparently, a sad and lonely character and had been getting the attention he sought by playing Russian roulette with his revolver. Russian roulette is the practice of loading only one bullet into the chamber of a revolver and spinning the cylinder and, without looking where the bullet is when the chamber has stopped spinning, close the gun. Having closed the gun the barrel is placed against the side of the head and the trigger pulled. In theory, when the cylinder is spun, the weight of the single bullet should mean that the cylinder stops spinning when the bullet is at the six o'clock position, and therefore, not in the firing position. The shocked fellow soldiers of the victim told me that the poor chap had been playing Russian roulette for several days and getting away with it, and at the same time getting the attention he so sadly craved.

Shortly afterwards, I took all the bullets out of my revolver bar one. I duly spun the cylinder, and before closing the gun when the cylinder had stopped spinning, looked to see where the bullet had stopped. It had stopped exactly in the position where, when the trigger was pulled, it would have been fired. I, therefore, would have played Russian roulette only once.

Chapter 14
An Ambush

During my year on active service in Cyprus, there were many occasions when Army personnel were ambushed. One such ambush remains particularly in my memory. When I was the duty medical officer, one night at about 3.30am, I was woken by the duty night corporal. He had been signalled that there had just been a report of a patrol of Royal Marines being ambushed in their Land Rover while patrolling in the Troodos Mountains. It was almost certain that there were severe casualties. Fortunately, one of the marines, the sergeant it turned out, was able to drive the vehicle, but it was not possible to know how long it would take the patrol with the wounded to arrive at the British Military Hospital.

Once warned by the duty corporal, I at once asked him to alert all the theatre staff while I woke Colonel John Watts to warn him of what was expected. After about half an hour of waiting with the theatre staff and Colonel Watts fully prepared, the Land Rover arrived.

One, the sergeant, I shall never forget. He had of course brought the whole patrol safely to the hospital. One bullet had passed through his beret, missing his head and another bullet through the pinna of his left ear. No one could have been closer to being killed than that whilst remaining virtually unscathed. Two marines had minor wounds, one to his arm and the other to his leg. In both cases, the wounds were readily sutured. The lieutenant however, was very badly wounded with several perforating wounds to his intestines. How fortunate that Colonel Watts was there to operate on him. During the complex operation, the lieutenant's wife had been informed, and she arrived at the hospital desperate to learn about her husband. I felt compelled to enter the operating theatre and enquire about the lieutenant's chances of surviving. Colonel Watts in his usual frank way told me that the odds for survival were not better than fifty-fifty. It was with great difficulty that I conveyed this news to the lieutenant's wife, being anxious to give her hope but not falsely so. How wonderful, thanks to Colonel Watt's great skill and experience, that the lieutenant recovered.

The warrant officer had a chest wound but his condition seemed satisfactory and he was put into the ward while waiting to be operated on. On checking him shortly afterwards, I found his condition had deteriorated badly and it was necessary to put a drip up on him while he waited to go to the theatre.

There was a remarkable sequel to the warrant officer. Once he had been operated on and made a partial recovery, he was flown back to the UK for further treatment. He was admitted to the men's surgical ward at St Thomas's Hospital, London where my sister, Hilary, was nursing. When she read his Army medical notes she recognised my writing, and told him that I was her brother. Whereupon he said that I had saved his life. Not true of course but I probably did a bit towards doing so – Colonel Watts doing the remaining 99%.

Chapter 15
Unwelcome Duties

As part of our medical training, during the three month pathology course, we were required to attend a minimum of three post mortem examinations. I certainly never wished to attend more than the minimum required to pass the course. I found them very unwelcome occasions. To my surprise, some students were anxious to attend more than the minimum, perhaps because they had an interest in becoming pathologists. Needless to say highly trained and skilled pathologists undertook the examinations.

A coroner will request a post mortem, among other reasons, when a death has resulted from a sudden, violent or unexpected cause. In 1956, the criteria, which applied in the UK, also applied in Cyprus. In the case of a serviceman being killed by EOKA in or near Nicosia, the local coroner requested a post mortem. It fell to John Turk, a fellow medical National Serviceman, and myself, to undertake these. It was the most unwelcome and stressful task and we took it in turns to do them. We were not trained pathologists and had to recall what we had learnt as students. The requirement of a post mortem is to establish the cause of death and for most EOKA victims this was usually all too obvious. A full examination was not required and it was a great relief to be able to avoid this.

Having confidently established the cause of death, we were required to write a report and send it to the coroner in

Nicosia. I cannot recall how many reports I sent, but however many it was, I never ever received an acknowledgement.

There was another extremely unwelcome duty, which some medical officers were ordered to do. It was to examine a prisoner who had been given a death sentence to confirm that he was fit to be hanged. It was with great relief that I was never ordered to undertake this bizarre and gruesome task. No medical training had ever been given to enable a doctor to do this. I talked to one of the unfortunate medical officers who had to do one of these examinations. I was told that the prisoner had to be judged both physically and mentally fit to be hanged. How fit did anyone have to be? This was a dreadful task, made more difficult by the fact that nearly all condemned prisoners did not speak English. What the mental state of a man condemned to be hanged is must be beyond calculation. I was just so grateful that I never had to undertake such a macabre duty.

Chapter 16
A Tragic Forest Fire

The Troodos mountain range is the largest in Cyprus, the highest peak of which is Mount Olympus. The range is situated in the central aspect of the island stretching across most of the western side. Scattered throughout the mountains are small villages and ancient Byzantine monasteries and churches. Vast areas of the mountain range are covered by forest. There are also copper mines, which are now mostly exhausted.

On the weekend of 17th June 1956, a forest fire broke out on the mountains. It spread rapidly, and the Cypriot fire brigade was unable to cope, especially as there was an extremely strong wind fanning the flames. Troops were sent to help but had no training for this hazard. Nineteen of them were burnt to death and many more badly wounded.

The fire spread so rapidly that it would leap across a valley. A soldier running away from the fire and having to go down one side and up the other would find that the flames had already gone across the top of the valley and reached the other side into which he was running. One party was saved, as their officer knew that a forest fire travelled about a foot and a half above ground. Instead of trying to run away his party lay face down on the ground. The fire passed safely over them leaving them uninjured.

The nineteen dead were brought back to the British Military Hospital and placed in a vacated hut for identification. The fire had so badly deformed most of them that they could only be identified by their dental records, which had to be obtained from the UK. Proof that the fire spread about a foot and a half above the ground was the fact that several of the bodies, although having had all the clothing burnt off them, still had boots and socks intact.

Working in the hut with the nineteen burnt bodies, checking the dental records and with the appalling smell, was a grim enough task for me. However, much more so for the two young RAMC corporals, whose conduct was magnificent.

The day after all was completed, the commanding officer called me in to see him. He told me that he had put in a special commendation for the two corporals, something that was well deserved by them. He then said that he would not be doing likewise for me, as he considered what I had done to be just part of my normal duties. I thanked him and duly left his office, not really quite sure what I had to be grateful for.

Chapter 17
Mistaken Orders

The narrow winding roads going to the top of the Troodos Mountains contained numerous hairpin bends. Vehicles had to be driven slowly, almost at a standstill round these. In such circumstances, vehicles made easy targets for EOKA and were extremely vulnerable to being ambushed.

Anyone high in the mountains could readily hear a vehicle slowly winding its way up the road, long before it reached the top. It gave EOKA members plenty of time to prepare an ambush. In the case of a car, not until it was visible could it be certain that it was occupied by Army personnel. The Army, however, frequently used 3-tonne lorries to transport troops. These vehicles made a characteristic high-pitched sound especially when in low gear. They could be heard high up in the mountains as they made their slow, but characteristically noisy way upwards. They made ideal targets for EOKA ambushes and initially these lorries and their personnel sustained casualties.

The casualty rate was significantly reduced when small groups of soldiers were transported in smaller vehicles whose engines were not readily identified. It was also decided to leave small groups of soldiers in the mountains to set ambushes for the EOKA members operating there.

An elite unit of the British Army was dispatched into the mountains. They were in the charge of a senior NCO.

Their purpose was to establish an ambush, for the EOKA fighters known to be there.

The NCO positioned the soldiers, well hidden for an ambush. He instructed them that they were to shoot the first person that walked into their ambush. For some unknown reason he walked away before eventually returning. The troops obeyed his orders explicitly and as he approached them they opened fire, killing him instantly.

When his body arrived at the military hospital we were all shocked and saddened that such an accident could have happened. It was some weeks later that I learnt that the NCO was extremely unpopular with the soldiers under his command. His orders to fire immediately at the first person returning were of course only stated to have been given after his death. I have always wondered, as a result of learning of his unpopularity, whether his death was due to an accident.

Chapter 18
Very Personal Tragedies

It was of course always deeply sad and upsetting whenever one of the soldiers serving in Cyprus was killed or badly wounded. Some such tragedies had extra dimensions added to them when the soldier who was killed was a friend. Each Army regiment had its own medical officer attached to it and, although from the Royal Army Medical Corps, such medical officers were essentially members of the regiment.

One such medical officer attached to the Blues and Royals during the EOKA campaign not only looked after the Army personnel in his regiment but also cared for wives of the regular officers. Married Army staff usually lived outside the regimental accommodation in rented houses. One afternoon, the medical officer had visited a sick wife at her home. He had just returned to his car after the visit when an EOKA gunman approached and shot him in the head at close range, killing him at once. He remained in his car for nearly two hours before his Army comrades discovered his body.

All of us at the British Military Hospital were deeply upset. We had got to know this man well, as he regularly visited the hospital to keep in touch with his fellow doctors and to visit any wounded soldiers from his regiment. He was a quiet, gentle and very caring person and doctor. An additional tragedy was that his wife was expecting a child, who was of course born fatherless.

Nicos Sampson was a well-known journalist in Cyprus, working for The Times of Cyprus. Although he travelled to many parts of the island, he worked mainly in and around Nicosia. One curious aspect of his reporting was how often he seemed to be near an EOKA murder when it happened. Only when the EOKA campaign was nearly over was it found out that, although a newspaper reporter, it was he who actually carried out, on behalf of EOKA, the murders he had so readily reported in his newspaper. It was confirmed after he was eventually arrested, that it was Nicos Sampson who had killed the medical officer of the Blues and Royals.

Approximately fifty years later, a good friend of our family happened to be talking about her god-daughter who, she said, had never known her father as he had been killed during the emergency in Cyprus. When I enquired further, it transpired that the father was the medical officer of the Guards Regiment. As the god-daughter had never known her father, a meeting was arranged for me to talk to her. It was a very emotional meeting for us both and I just hope I was able to convey to her what a wonderful man her father had been.

Another particularly sad death was that of a young Royal Marines Officer. On a Tuesday of the week in which he was to be married, an EOKA hand grenade was tossed into the back of the Land Rover in which he was travelling, killing him instantly. The hand grenades used by EOKA were made from a section of metal piping with a metal plate welded on sealing one end, and a pipe end piece screwed on the other end. A hole was drilled to allow entry of the four-second fuse. Fragments of metal were placed inside with the explosive to maximise the destructive effect when the grenade exploded. They were horribly effective, as was so sadly shown in the death of this unfortunate young man in the week of his wedding.

Chapter 19
Blood Transfusion

In the United Kingdom, blood for transfusion is available to hospitals from the National Blood Transfusion Service. In hospitals where the blood is used it is not necessary, therefore, to have means of obtaining blood from donors. The National Blood Transfusion Service makes the blood available. This is in contrast to the situation the medical services of the Army faced in Cyprus. The only blood available for transfusion had to be obtained by the medical services at the British Military Hospital from donor soldiers in Cyprus.

Blood once taken from a donor remains fit for transfusing for up to three weeks. After which time it has to be discarded. It was never possible to be certain how much blood would be needed at any one time. If a large stock of blood had been stored a considerable amount of it might have been wasted depending on the demand.

In order to avoid taking blood from soldiers and subsequently having it wasted, a donor panel was organised amongst the troops in such a way that blood could be obtained at very short notice at the time of need, rather than from a large store which would be subject to waste. Initially, only four pints of universal donor blood was routinely stored to be available for immediate use. Towards the end of 1955, for the first time, three donor panels were established among the troops. One panel for routine operations, other than for casualties from EOKA activities, was established among troops stationed some distance outside Nicosia. A second panel for more urgent need was set up among troops stationed in Nicosia, and the panel for the most acute emergencies was established among staff working in the British Military Hospital itself. They were immediately available when severely wounded soldiers arrived. Within half an hour of an urgent call for blood from the operating theatre, it was possible to have obtained blood from a donor on the hospital emergency panel, cross-matched it with the recipient's blood, and have it ready for use. While the theatre staff waited for half an hour for the newly obtained blood, one of the four stored bottles was available for use immediately.

In early 1956, the number of severe casualties from EOKA activities increased considerably. On several occasions large amounts of blood had to be issued over very short periods for severely injured soldiers. In April 1956, during a twenty-four hour period, it was necessary to bleed forty-eight donors with forty-two pints of blood being issued. On another occasion, during only a seven hour period, forty-two donors had to be bled for badly wounded soldiers admitted, when a bomb had been thrown into their vehicle.

My colleague John Turk, undertook the blood grouping and cross-matching of the blood. To his great credit, in spite of the extreme urgency and stress of his responsibilities, no wrongly tested or labelled blood occurred. My commitment was to bleed the donors and to ensure they were all right when the bleeding was completed. Each donor was then given a can of beer as a "thank you" and I became popular as it fell to me to hand the cans out to the soldiers.

To give an indication of the amount of blood needed at times, of the one hundred soldiers transfused during 1956, twenty-six required at least five pints of blood, eleven over ten pints, and five had twenty pints of blood or just over. During all this time there were no reactions attributable to the transfusion of incompatible blood. Although 'self-praise is no recommendation', this was a great tribute to all the medical and orderly staff involved.

In the autumn of 1956, during the build up to the Suez Canal attack, the British Military Hospital was designated to be the principle medical source for treating casualties from the invasion. From what was already known about the difficulties of producing enough blood for casualties from the EOKA campaign, it would clearly not have been possible to cope with any further demand for blood for casualties from the Suez invasion. In view of this, prior to the invasion, a large quantity of blood was flown out from the UK for us to store ready for use when the consequences of the invasion occurred. Unfortunately, this large supply of blood arrived more than three weeks before the invasion took place and it all had to be discarded. Thank goodness the people who donated the blood never knew what happened to it. No further blood supplies were ever sent from the UK, and fortunately, no more than five casualties arrived in Cyprus from the Suez invasion. Only years later did I learn that there were in fact many casualties, but instead of being flown back to the British Military Hospital, Nicosia, they were taken by helicopter to the Royal Navy ships anchored off Port Said.

An account of the blood transfusion service established by John Turk and myself was published in the Journal of the RAMC in 1957. Its heading is "The Development and Organisation of the Army Blood Bank in Cyprus, August 1955–August 1956 by Captain J A Lunn RAMC and Captain J L Turk RAMC".

Chapter 20
Embalming
The Saddest of Requests

In recent years, the bodies of members of the Armed Forces who have been killed in conflicts abroad have been flown back to the United Kingdom for burial. The sad sight of a coffin draped in a Union Jack being carried by bearers from an RAF transport plane has been an all too familiar recent sight. In contrast to present times, deceased soldiers in 1956 were not returned to the UK for internment, but buried in a military cemetery in the land where they had been killed. In Cyprus, burials took place at Wayne's Keep Military Cemetery just outside Nicosia.

As is customary in hot climates, the burials took place within a day or two. For most grieving relatives it had to be accepted that their sons or husbands would never return to their homeland. The relatives were told that if they could find the very high cost of having the body returned to the UK, arrangements could be made for this to take place. In some cases, after a few days, a request would come from relatives for a body of a deceased soldier to be flown home.

By the time these requests were received, the burial of the soldier had already taken place. It was necessary therefore for the body to be exhumed. This task fell to the comrades of the deceased and to an Army medical officer who was required to be present at the exhumation. I was designated to be that officer. Just after dawn, in order to be as peaceful and unnoticed as possible, the party would assemble at Wayne's Keep Military cemetery. Four of the buried soldier's comrades would proceed on the saddest of tasks. In complete silence, they would dig down to remove their friend's coffin.

The exhumed body would be returned to the Military Hospital. Regulations at that time required that a body being flown in an aircraft had to be embalmed and placed in a lead-lined coffin. No one at the Military Hospital had any knowledge or experience of embalming, but it fell to John Turk and myself to learn how to do this and carry out the task. We managed to find the necessary solutions, which had to be prepared and then injected into the main arteries of the body in order to ensure its preservation.

There were several occasions when such embalming had to be carried out. However much I was saddened by these occasions, my feelings were nothing compared to those of the young comrades of the deceased who had to carry out the exhumation. I am sure it is something they were never to forget. I only hope they have been able to come to terms with what they had to do, and to realise how much they helped the family of their diseased comrade to have his body home.

Chapter 21
Jerusalem

In early July 1956, the Roman Catholic padre at the hospital was able to organise a weekend trip to Jerusalem. There were ten vacancies available; and I was fortunate to obtain one, and at the same time arrange to have Army leave.

The padre beforehand gave us a brief synopsis of the history of Jerusalem, not an easy task, as the city probably has the most complex and detailed history of any in the world. The Old City is designated a World Heritage site, and is the Holy City of Christians, Jews and Muslims.

Archaeological evidence suggests that the first settlements began between 4500 and 3500 BC. The Canaanite religion was established; and by the 17th century BC, the Canaanites had built the first of many massive stone structures. It is estimated that they built a wall 26 feet high using boulders weighing 4–5 tons. In 1550–1400 BC, the city came under Egyptian control. The Israelite history began in 1000 BC when King David sacked the city. He later built the Temple of Solomon.

In the first century BC, Jerusalem was part of the Roman Empire and became a Roman province. The Jewish population rebelled against this occupation and temporarily regained control of the city. In due course under Emperor Titus, the Romans recaptured the city and destroyed many buildings including the Temple. Today, the retaining wall of this holy building remains and is called the Western Wall, sometimes the Wailing Wall.

Following the decline of the Roman Empire, the city was ruled by Muslims until retaken by the Crusaders in 1099 AD. Although the Crusaders were acting in the name of Christianity, it is recorded that they inflicted the most appalling atrocities on the population. The city was later captured by the Ottoman Empire in 1516 AD, and ruled by that empire until 1917 when General Allenby retook the city.

In later years, Jerusalem was divided into the old east side under Jordanian control, and the more modern western side under the Israelis. In the Six Day War in 1967, the city became united again under Israeli control and remains so today.

The Roman Catholic padre somehow managed to arrange the RAF to fly us in a Dakota aircraft. The Dakota has been one of the most famous of American aircraft. First produced in 1943, it became available to the RAF in 1945. It has been renowned for its safety and reliability and could still be flying today. Our accommodation in Jerusalem was in a Catholic monastery. This was somewhat austere but perfectly adequate. We each had our own room. There was one long narrow dining table with benches for seating.

During the weekend visit, we had the privilege of seeing the most sacred and treasured sites in the city. Our Roman Catholic padre was well acquainted with Jerusalem as this was not his first visit. He was a superb guide. It is difficult to say which of the holy places was the most special and moving, but perhaps being in the Garden of Gethsemane was the one giving the greatest sense of the past. In the Garden, some of the olive trees were at least 2,000 years old, and we could have been looking at the very same ones that Christ would have seen.

At the end of our visit, we assembled at what was a very simple airfield in those days and waited outside on a sandy area for the Dakota to return. The time for its expected arrival passed; but about fifteen minutes later, after an anxious wait, we could see a pin-sized object in the cloudless sky. As the speck came nearer we knew that it was the Dakota coming to take us back to Cyprus.

Chapter 22
Saint Hilarion Castle

On one occasion when Maureen and I were able to have time off from her nursing and my Army commitments at the same time, we decided to visit Saint Hilarion castle. Before going, we were able to learn much of the past history of the site and to have a much deeper feeling for the remarkable history of the castle.

The castle was built on the Kyrenia mountain range on the north Cyprus coast. The site gave the castle command of the pass road from Kyrenia to Nicosia. It was named after the hermit monk, Saint Hilarion who first settled there. One account of his life claims that he lived and died in a cave on the mountain. In later years, following his death, a monastery and church were built at the site where he spent his austere life.

An alternative account claims that earlier in his life, Saint Hilarion was an abbot in Palestine where he founded a monastery following his conversion to Christianity after studying at Alexandria. He then travelled widely in the Middle East, and gained fame for performing miracles. He apparently took no pleasure in the crowds he attracted and sought a quieter life. He travelled to Cyprus and settled near Paphos where he died at the age of eighty. He was buried close to Paphos, but at a later date his relics were taken to today's castle site where they were buried.

Whichever story is nearer the truth, his name will always be remembered at the castle.

The original monastery and church were in later years developed into the castle. The exact date is not known, but the castle was almost certainly built by the eleventh century AD. The Emperor Alexis 1, by then, had captured the castle to strengthen his hold on Cyprus.

During the Crusades in 1191, Richard the Lionheart on his way to Palestine invaded Cyprus and sought to capture Saint Hilarion Castle. His second in command, Guy de Lusignan, undertook the assault as Richard had become sick and remained in Nicosia to recover. The castle was captured by Guy de Lusignan. He subsequently retained control of Cyprus when King Richard, recovered from his illness, continued on his way to the Holy Land.

Further conflicts took place when the Emperor Frederick II, also travelling to Palestine, landed at Limassol and demanded that he had control of Cyprus, and, of course, Saint Hilarion Castle. His justification for this was on the grounds that Guy de Lusignan had obtained his crown from Emperor Frederick's father, Henry VI of France in 1197.

Anticipating the Emperor's assault on the castle, the women and children were sent to safety and the castle's food supplies adequately increased. A stalemate ensued and the Emperor and Guy de Lusignan called a truce. United together, they both embarked on the crusade and left Cyprus for the Holy Land. For at least the next 140 years, there was peace on the island; until 1489 when the Venetians invaded and captured the island. They relied for the defence of the island on Kyrenia, Nicosia and Famagusta. Saint Hilarion castle became neglected and fell into disrepair. In much later years, this neglect was halted when the historic importance of the castle was appreciated.

Today Saint Hilarion Castle is a tourist attraction, but in 1956 mass tourism had not begun. When Maureen and I climbed the rocks to reach the castle remains, we were entirely on our own. Complete silence except for the gentle sound of the sea below. We were able to enjoy the beautiful view across the Mediterranean Sea in the direction of Turkey. It didn't seem right to have a picnic exactly in the castle precincts, where so many human tragedies and events had happened. We walked halfway down the rocks before settling down for our picnic.

Our visit to Saint Hilarion Castle has remained a treasured memory. We were able to be where so many historic figures had lived and fought and where many had died.

A strange incident took place after we had left Cyprus. A British holidaymaker had taken photographs of Saint Hilarion Castle. When the photographs were developed, quite clearly on more than one of them taken of the top of the castle, a white figure of a human being could be seen standing on the edge of the castle wall. This was the exact spot where past traitors were thrown over the wall to their inevitable deaths.

Chapter 23
Outstanding Courage

During the course of the year 1956, there were, among the soldiers and Cypriot population, numerous acts of courage and selfless consideration for others. In addition, there were outstanding examples of devotion to duty in the hardest of circumstances and a sense of humour displayed while suffering great hardship or severe adversity.

The Army often employed civilians from the Cypriot population because of a shortage of Army personnel. One such need was to employ Cypriot drivers for Land Rovers transporting troops around the island.

One afternoon an emergency call came to the Military Hospital that an Army Land Rover had been ambushed about twenty five miles along the Nicosia road to Limassol, resulting in several casualties. With the narrow road obstructed at times by a farmer moving his cattle, it took nearly forty minutes to reach the ambushed vehicle. It was the usual sad and destructive scene. A dead sergeant was slumped in the front passenger seat and the Cypriot driver was still in the driver's seat, clearly badly wounded.

The dead sergeant was placed on the top bunk in the ambulance and the Cypriot in the lower bunk beneath. I sat on the shallow ledge of the ambulance floor close to the Cypriot. Although he was badly wounded with gunshot wounds to his abdomen, he remained conscious. He had no concern for himself but kept asking me, "How is my friend the sergeant?"

To avoid causing him more stress, I told him that the sergeant was wounded but unconscious. Telling the Cypriot the truth would have caused him so much sadness, and it seemed right to avoid doing so. During the journey back to Nicosia, the badly wounded Cypriot asked me several more times how his friend the sergeant was and I felt bound to give the same reply.

Two days later I enquired how he was getting on. It was tragic to hear that he had died that morning. He had been totally without thought for himself although so badly injured. His only thoughts had been for the sergeant and the memory of this wonderful Cypriot is one never to be forgotten.

A second unsettling incident occurred in an RAF unit. One of the Cypriots working there was either an EOKA member or someone acting in fear of not doing EOKA's bidding. A bomb was placed under the billiards table in the airmen's mess. It was timed to explode when the game was being played in the evening. Tragically, the bomb exploded exactly as planned, and one poor RAF ground crew had a leg blown off and the other severely wounded. Fortunately, thanks to Colonel Watt's superb surgical skills the badly wounded leg was saved.

A third incident took place out of doors. Some soldiers in a detachment of the Highland Light Infantry were able to have some recreation by playing football on a pitch near a Cypriot village. There was a well situated close to the pitch. After playing football in extremely hot conditions, the soldiers would gather round the well to refresh themselves. Unfortunately, this gathering had been observed by EOKA. They managed to plant a bomb inside the well, which exploded when the soldiers were gathered round it after their game of football. Although none were killed, there were dreadful casualties among them.

A further memory is of a courageous young soldier. In the early morning of a day on which I was the duty medical officer, a bomb explosion had injured a young Scottish National Serviceman's leg so badly that the leg had to be amputated above the knee. As usual when duty medical officer, I would be doing a last minute ward round in the evening to check that nothing unexpected was happening to any of the wounded soldiers. I knew that the first casualty to be seen would be the young Scotsman. I wondered what on earth I could say that would make any sense or be of comfort to him. As I approached the foot of his bed, still at a loss, his face broke into a broad grin and, speaking before I could say anything, said, "No more marching for me, thank goodness!"

What a fantastic person. It was as if he had sensed my uncertainty and was thoughtful enough to save me from it. It was he who helped me and not the other way round. Needless to say, after ensuring that he was not in pain and felt as comfortable as possible in the circumstances, we had a delightful chat. What an inspiration to have met him.

Chapter 24
Salamis

A visit to Salamis was another wonderful opportunity to see a site of great antiquity and interest. Salamis is an ancient city on the east coast of Cyprus at the mouth of the River Pedieos. The city's history stretches back many centuries as far as 1100 BC. In Roman times, the city was part of the Roman province of Cilicia.

Salamis was originally the capital of Cyprus but was later replaced by Paphos, where the Roman governor of Cilicia had his headquarters. Nicosia has of course now replaced Paphos as the island capital. The emperors of Rome, especially Hadrian, considered Salamis to be an important part of their empire, and did a great deal to restore the public buildings. These included a gymnasium, amphitheatre and public baths.

The apostle Paul, travelled from Antioch in Syria to Salamis to proclaim Christianity in Salamis and the rest of the island. Paul and Barnabas founded the Church of Cyprus, but Barnabas made enemies and was stoned to death in Salamis in 61 AD.

After the decline of the Roman Empire, Salamis became less important and many buildings were allowed to fall into disrepair. This was accelerated in the Middle Ages, when ancient buildings were looted to use their stones to build castles. Fortunately, a great deal of ancient Salamis became buried under sand, which helped to preserve many remaining buildings from destruction.

In the nineteenth century, it became recognised that more should be done to preserve and protect ancient ruins, and archaeological work began at Salamis. Against this historic background, a small group of us stationed at the BMH Nicosia obtained leave to make a day trip to Salamis. Remains of Roman buildings were close to the shore, and over the centuries, the sea had clearly encroached on the land. Some pillars were still standing, but many had fallen. Wearing watertight goggles when swimming in the sea, items of pottery from ancient times, probably Roman, were visible on the seabed. We left them undisturbed where they had probably rested for hundreds of years.

The EOKA campaign meant that it was wise for two of our party to stay on the shore to be on guard against any danger while the others swam. After the two on safety duty had swapped with those who had first swum, we departed for the BMH Nicosia. A fascinating part of history had been seen and also remnants of outstanding Roman architecture. We had stood where Paul the Apostle had landed from his journey from Antioch in Syria and where poor Barnabas had met his death. We left with much to reflect on.

Chapter 25
The Suez Crisis and Bahrain

With French planning and, initially, British reluctance, the Suez Canal was constructed. It linked the Mediterranean with the Red Sea, saving the long voyage round Africa in order to reach the Far East. One of the great geniuses behind the project was the Frenchman, Ferdinand de Lessops. Construction of the canal lasted about ten years, between 1859 and 1869. Once the canal was completed, Britain and France retained control and profited from the dues paid by the ships sailing through it.

In 1956, President Gamal Nasser of Egypt nationalised the canal, thus taking control away from Britain and France. Against nearly all world opinion, Britain and France planned to attack Egypt in order to regain control of the Suez Canal.

Arab opinion was particularly opposed to the intention to retake the canal. Some Arab states in the Persian Gulf declared that they would massacre every British ex-patriot in the Gulf if Britain and France went ahead with their intention to retake the canal. In order to help safeguard against this happening, a detachment of the Gloucester Regiment was dispatched to Bahrain. The detachment arrived without medical cover and I was posted to Bahrain to provide this.

The RAF flew me from Cyprus to Bahrain, stopping at a staging post in Iraq en route. One day, not long after arriving in Bahrain, following a midday meal in the officers' mess, I was driven in a Land Rover along the desert road back to the tented accommodation a mile or two away. An approaching vehicle, instead of slowing down, continued driving towards us and at the last minute, in order to avoid an accident, my driver had to give way and turned sharply to the left. Unfortunately, this resulted in the near side wheel of the Land Rover hitting a boulder. The vehicle became out of control and we realised we had a puncture. This is all I can remember until finding myself kneeling on the desert sand with blood streaming from my head and forming a pool on the sand. I had no recollection of going through the windscreen.

After asking the driver to put first aid dressings on my head to control the bleeding, he discovered there were none in the vehicle. He then ran back to the camp from where we had just come to get help. I tried to stop the bleeding from my head but was unable to do so. An artery had been severed and I could not control the blood loss. I truly felt my life was about to end when miraculously a car driven by a young woman working for the Foreign Office in Bahrain arrived. Seeing me she stopped, helped me into her car, and drove straight back to the Army base. Here I received appropriate first aid treatment before being taken to the Bahrain General Hospital. I had marvellous treatment there by the medical superintendent, Dr Snow. All wounds were sutured and I had to have a blood transfusion to replace the amount I had lost. While still in bed, because the Land Rover was a complete write off, there was an Army court of enquiry. Rather precipitately, it was held at the foot of my bed. Two Army officers officiated with the poor driver of the vehicle standing by the bed. After a series of questions, the officer conducting the enquiry asked a final one. "Did I consider that the driver of the Land Rover was

76

responsible for the accident?" One look at the poor driver gave me the clear answer. "No he was not".

After ten days in the Bahrain hospital, I was flown back to Cyprus, and shortly afterwards back to the UK as my two years National Service were nearly over. Because of the severity of my facial wounds I required plastic surgery to improve their appearance. The operation was successfully performed at Roehampton Hospital. Now many years later the once prominent wounds are hardly visible.

One lasting regret I have about this incident is that I was flown back to Cyprus without ever knowing and thanking the young woman who saved my life.

Chapter 26
The Territorial Army

After two years in the Regular Army, National Servicemen were required to do a period in the Territorial Army. I was posted to the 57th (Middlesex) General Hospital RAMC (TA) in Harrow. The unit was a potential hospital, in that, it had nearly all the necessary personnel to staff one. Unfortunately, the only thing we didn't have was a hospital.

The commanding officer was a very distinguished London surgeon and the general personnel were mostly practising doctors or medical orderlies. There was little need for additional relevant military training. We did, however, have some training in nerve gas warfare, which I found most depressing. We were told that just one drop of nerve gas touching the skin would be fatal. We were comforted by being told that there would probably be a four-minute warning of a gas attack during which time we would be able to cover ourselves in protective clothing. This consisted of trousers and a hooded cape to be put on over our existing uniforms. The material of these garments would prevent the nerve gas passing through. It is always difficult to pull trousers over Army boots and it was necessary for me to have an extra large protective pair. The Army corporal making a record of our clothing needs misheard "extra large" for "extra small", and my documents recorded that I would be issued with the latter size. It was difficult enough to put the correct size on, but beyond possibility to put the extra small size pair on. I would have been the first casualty of a nerve gas attack, which, thank goodness, has never happened. In spite of repeatedly notifying the establishment that I needed an extra large and not an extra small pair of protective trousers, the record was never altered. Perhaps someone didn't like me!

Each year, our TA unit had a fortnight's camp. On one occasion, we were required to staff a military hospital somewhere on the south coast of England. We replaced the regular staff and had to be ready to undertake any medical care needed for nearby regular Army troops.

On the second day of our commitment, a young regular soldier arrived with clear signs and symptoms of acute appendicitis. Our distinguished London surgeon was anxious to demonstrate his surgical skills and remove the offending appendix. The only problem was who would act as the anaesthetist? This was one speciality our unit lacked. During my first year after leaving the regular Army, I had a traineeship in general practice in Tonbridge, Kent. The senior partner in the practice had experience of surgery and performed operations in the local cottage hospital. Another partner had anaesthetic experience and provided the necessary cover for the operations. I always went to assist the senior partner when he was operating. I was also able to acquire some knowledge of giving anaesthetics. It must be remembered that anaesthetic techniques were not as refined in those days as they are today.

My slender experience of giving anaesthetics must somehow have reached the ears of our commanding officer. I was ordered to act as his anaesthetist when he performed the appendectomy on the young soldier. The operation only took about twenty minutes but it was the longest twenty minutes of my life. I was able to remember the essentials of anaesthesia for such a simple operation, but adequate experience I did not have. When the surgeon had put the final closing skin suture in, he turned to thank me. I was just so relieved that everything had gone well, but I vowed never ever to give another anaesthetic.

Later that day, I went to the surgical ward to see if all was well with the soldier. He was fast asleep and clearly comfortable; so all, to my great relief, was well.

Chapter 27
Reflections

Very few young doctors, qualified for only a year, wished to interrupt their medical experience with the commitment to do two years National Service in the Armed Forces. I was no exception. I believed that two years in the Army would add nothing to my medical knowledge and would simply delay me from developing my medical career. How wrong I was to have had these doubts!

During my two years National Service in the Royal Army Medical Corps, I was privileged to meet and at times help, many courageous, selfless and caring people. People whose qualities I hoped that I could emulate should I ever be in the circumstances that they found themselves in. When faced with badly wounded soldiers, I felt humbled to witness fortitude and courage in the way they coped with their wounds. The young Scotsman who had just had his badly wounded leg amputated, smiling, as he said, "No more marching for me, thank goodness!" No self-pity whatsoever. What a wonderful person to have met. I learnt the strengths that people could summon in extreme adversity.

Colonel John Watts, the distinguished World War II surgeon, who saved the lives of many severely wounded soldiers, inspired all who worked under him. I was one such fortunate person. His leadership and experience were an inspiration to us all. However daunting the task ahead,

Colonel Watts always left us in no doubt that everything would work out. How privileged I was to have known him.

Many years after leaving the Army, it has been of great interest to reminisce with others of my generation who also did National Service and to exchange experiences. One interesting and slightly amusing common factor has been that everyone in this category has said that they never forgot their service identity number. How true. Mine was "439324" and please believe me, I have not made it up!

It only remains for me to say: "Thank you National Service."

The author's army group intake in January 1955 (author back row, third from left).

Embarking on the Empire Ken at Southampton

The author and the Sphinx

Officers' mess at the British Military Hospital, Fayid, Egypt

En route to Ain Sukhna to see the picturesque coral

Warning of mine dangers at 9 Bad at Abu Sultan

Land Rover with metal spine in front to guard against wires strung across roads

Imprint found in the sand of a boat used to transport stones across the Nile for pyramid construction

Stretchers on Land Rover for transporting wounded

Salamis and remains of Roman buildings

Roman remains at Salamis, possibly of communal baths

Saint Hilarion Castle seen from the approach road

Sergeant of the Camel Corps

Preparing to mount...

Honorary member!

*View from the King's
Apartments at Saint Hilarion
Castle*

*Kyrenia showing local graffiti
support for EOKA*

*The Church of the Nativity.
The original arched entrance
can be seen blocked in to stop
marauding horsemen*

*The Garden of Gethsemane with some olive trees at least two
thousand years old*

A bomb casualty at the British Military Hospital, Nicosia being taken from the rescue helicopter

Renault car at Xeros and author, Maureen and good friend, Glyn Bennett

Renault lent by Ian Sparling